Workforce Mojo: Unleash Singapore's Success.

By Carol Sichembo.

Introduction

- Briefly introduce Singapore's economic transformation and its focus on workforce development.
- Highlight the concept of "Workforce Mojo" - a high-performing, engaged, and skilled workforce.
- Explain why investing in your workforce is critical for business success in today's competitive world.

Part 1: The Singapore Story

- Chapter 1: From Humble Beginnings to Economic Powerhouse - Singapore's pre-independence challenges and the early strategies adopted by the government.
- Chapter 2: Building the Foundation - Focus on education, infrastructure development, and creating a business-friendly environment.
- Chapter 3: The Skills Revolution - How Singapore shifted from a manufacturing base to a knowledge

economy and the corresponding workforce development strategies.
- Chapter 4: The Singapore Advantage - Key takeaways from Singapore's approach - focus on lifelong learning, meritocracy, and building a strong government-industry partnership.

Part 2: Unleashing Workforce Mojo in Your Organization

- Chapter 5: Assessing Your Workforce Needs - Identifying skill gaps, understanding future trends, and setting goals for workforce development.
- Chapter 6: Building a Culture of Learning - Creating a supportive environment that encourages continuous learning and development.
- Chapter 7: Investing in Training and Development Programs - Tailoring programs to address specific skill needs and career aspirations.

- Chapter 8: Fostering Engagement and Motivation - Strategies to keep employees engaged, motivated, and satisfied in their roles.
- Chapter 9: Measuring Success - Tracking the impact of your workforce development initiatives and making adjustments as needed.

Part 3: Case Studies and Industry Examples

- Chapter 10: Companies That Get It Right - Showcase real-world examples of organizations that have successfully invested in their workforce and achieved significant results. (Include companies from various industries)
- Chapter 11: Challenges and Opportunities - Discuss potential roadblocks to implementing a strong workforce development strategy and how to overcome them.
- Chapter 12: The Future of Work - Explore emerging trends in workforce development and how to prepare your organization for the future.

Conclusion

- Recap the key takeaways from the book and emphasize the importance of continuous investment in workforce development for sustainable success.
- Provide actionable steps for readers to take and resources for further exploration.
- How to Adapt the Singapore Model to Your Context - Discuss how to take inspiration from Singapore's approach but tailor it to the specific needs and circumstances of your organization and country.

Introduction: Unleashing the Workforce Mojo - The Singapore Story and Your Company's Success

Imagine a nation transformed. Just a few decades ago, Singapore was a developing country struggling with high unemployment and a lack of resources. Today, it stands as a beacon of economic prosperity, boasting a highly skilled workforce and a world-class standard of living. This remarkable transformation wasn't driven by an abundance of natural resources or sheer luck. It was fueled by a powerful vision and a relentless commitment to one key factor: **investing in its people**.

This book is an invitation to unlock the same potential within your organization. We'll delve into the fascinating story of Singapore's rise, exploring the strategies they implemented to cultivate a workforce brimming with "Workforce Mojo." This isn't just about acquiring a specific skill set; it's about building a culture of continuous learning, engagement, and a deep well of motivation that propels individuals and businesses to achieve extraordinary things.

The Workforce Mojo Advantage

Think of Workforce Mojo as the secret sauce that separates high-performing companies from the rest. It's the intangible force that ignites creativity, fuels innovation, and fosters a relentless drive for excellence. It's a workforce that isn't just competent, but passionate, adaptable, and eager to tackle any challenge that comes their way.

Why Invest in Your Workforce Now?

The world of work is undergoing a seismic shift. Technological advancements are automating tasks at an unprecedented rate, and the skills that were once in high demand are rapidly becoming obsolete. To thrive in this ever-evolving landscape, companies need a workforce that can not only keep pace with change but actively embrace it.

Investing in your workforce isn't just about staying afloat; it's about seizing the opportunities that this transformation presents. By nurturing a culture of lifelong learning and empowering your employees to develop their skills, you'll be well-positioned to:

- **Become an innovation powerhouse:** A workforce brimming with Workforce Mojo is a breeding ground for creative solutions. They'll be constantly seeking ways to improve processes, develop new products and services, and stay ahead of the curve.
- **Enhance your adaptability:** The business landscape is no longer static. Companies that can adapt quickly to changing market conditions and customer demands will be the ones that survive and prosper. A workforce equipped with the right skills and mindset will be the engine that drives this adaptability.

- **Attract and retain top talent:** In today's competitive talent market, the best employees have their pick of opportunities. Companies that prioritize workforce development will be seen as desirable employers, attracting high-caliber individuals who are eager to learn, grow, and contribute their talents.
- **Boost employee engagement and satisfaction:** When employees feel valued and invested in, they're more likely to be engaged, motivated, and satisfied in their roles. This translates to increased productivity, lower turnover rates, and a more positive work environment.
- **Unlock the potential of your entire organization:** When every member of your workforce is operating at their peak potential, the collective impact is phenomenal. Imagine the synergy that arises when a team of highly skilled and motivated individuals come together to achieve a common goal. The possibilities are truly limitless.

The Singapore Miracle: A Blueprint for Success

Singapore's story serves as a powerful testament to the transformative power of investing in your workforce. We'll explore their journey in detail, examining the key pillars of their strategy:

- **A Relentless Focus on Education:** Singapore recognized that a skilled workforce is the bedrock of a thriving economy. They invested heavily in education, ensuring their citizens had access to quality learning opportunities from a young age.
- **Building a Culture of Lifelong Learning:** Education wasn't seen as a one-time event in Singapore. The government actively fostered a culture of continuous learning, encouraging individuals to upgrade their skills throughout their careers.
- **Meritocracy and Recognizing Talent:** Singapore created a system that rewarded hard work, talent, and

a desire to learn. This meritocratic approach ensured that the most capable individuals were given the opportunities to excel.

- **Developing a Strong Government-Industry Partnership:** The government and private sector worked hand-in-hand to identify skill gaps and develop targeted training programs that met the specific needs of the economy.

Your Company's Workforce Mojo Journey Begins Here

This book is your roadmap to unlocking the immense potential within your organization. We'll provide a step-by-step guide on how to cultivate Workforce Mojo, from assessing your current workforce needs to building a culture of learning and implementing effective training programs. We'll also explore inspiring case studies of companies that have successfully harnessed the power of their workforce to achieve remarkable results.

By the end of this journey, you'll be equipped with the knowledge, strategies, and tools to unleash the Workforce Mojo within your organization. Get ready to witness a transformation – a transformation that will propel your company.

Chapter 1: From Humble Beginnings to Economic Powerhouse: Singapore's Journey of Transformation

Singapore's story is one of remarkable transformation. This tiny island nation, with limited natural resources, has emerged as a global leader in trade, finance, and innovation. This chapter explores Singapore's pre-independence challenges and the early strategies adopted by the government that laid the foundation for its phenomenal success.

Pre-Independence Challenges

Prior to gaining independence in 1965, Singapore faced several significant challenges:

- **Limited Land and Resources:** Singapore is a small island nation with scarce land and natural resources. This posed a significant constraint for economic development.

- **High Unemployment:** Following the departure of the British military in the early 1960s, Singapore faced a high unemployment rate, threatening social stability.
- **Lack of Infrastructure:** The country's infrastructure was underdeveloped, hindering connectivity and limiting opportunities for trade and investment.
- **Ethnic Diversity:** Singapore's population is a multi-ethnic mix of Chinese, Malays, Indians, and Eurasians. This diversity, while a source of strength, also presented challenges in forging a national identity and social cohesion.

Early Government Strategies

The newly independent government of Singapore, led by Prime Minister Lee Kuan Yew, embarked on a series of ambitious strategies to address these challenges and propel the nation towards economic prosperity. Here are some key initiatives:

- **Export-Oriented Industrialization:** The government prioritized export-oriented industrialization. They actively attracted foreign investment by offering tax breaks, establishing free trade zones, and building world-class infrastructure. This transformed Singapore into a global hub for manufacturing and trade.
- **Investment in Education and Skills Development:** Recognizing the importance of human capital, the government heavily invested in education and skills development. They implemented a meritocratic education system that equipped Singaporeans with the skills needed to compete in the global economy.
- **Focus on Public Service Efficiency:** The government established a reputation for clean and efficient governance. They built a strong and meritocratic civil service that attracted talented individuals and fostered a business-friendly environment.
- **Maintaining Social Order and Stability:** The government prioritized social order and stability, seen

as essential for economic development. They implemented pragmatic social policies that addressed racial and income inequality, fostering a sense of national unity.

The Impact of Early Strategies

These early strategies by the Singaporean government yielded significant results:

- **Rapid Economic Growth:** Singapore experienced rapid economic growth, transforming from a developing nation to a high-income, developed economy within a few decades.
- **Reduced Unemployment:** The unemployment rate fell dramatically, and Singapore developed a skilled and competitive workforce.
- **Improved Infrastructure:** The government invested heavily in infrastructure development, creating a world-class transportation network, port facilities, and telecommunications systems.

- **Social Upward Mobility:** Investment in education and social policies facilitated social mobility, allowing Singaporeans to climb the economic ladder and improve their quality of life.

Conclusion

Singapore's journey from a resource-poor nation to an economic powerhouse is a testament to the power of strategic planning, investment in human capital, and good governance. The early strategies adopted by the government laid a strong foundation for the country's continued success in the decades to come. The following chapters will delve deeper into specific aspects of Singapore's development model, exploring areas like education, industrial development, and attracting foreign direct investment.

Chapter 2: Building the Foundation - Lessons from Singapore's Ascent

Singapore's economic miracle wasn't a stroke of luck. It was meticulously constructed, brick by brick, on a foundation of three key elements: a world-class education system, robust infrastructure development, and a meticulously crafted business-friendly environment. Let's delve deeper into each of these pillars and explore how they fueled Singapore's transformation.

Education: The Cornerstone of a Skilled Workforce

Singapore's leaders understood a fundamental truth: a nation's prosperity hinges on the quality of its human capital. In the early days of independence, the country faced a significant challenge – a large, young population with limited educational opportunities. The government embarked on an ambitious plan to transform the education landscape.

- **Investing in Quality**: Significant resources were poured into building a strong public education system. Schools were equipped with modern facilities, and rigorous curriculums were implemented, emphasizing not just rote learning but also critical thinking, problem-solving, and adaptability – skills crucial for success in the modern economy.
- **Nurturing Every Talent**: The system wasn't designed as a one-size-fits-all mold. Students were assessed based on their strengths and aptitudes, and various pathways were available – from academic tracks leading to prestigious universities to vocational training programs that equipped individuals with industry-specific skills.
- **Lifelong Learning**: Education wasn't viewed as a finite process ending with graduation. Singapore actively fostered a culture of lifelong learning through skills development programs, professional certifications, and readily available adult education opportunities. This ensured their workforce remained

relevant and adaptable in the face of rapid technological advancements.

Building the Arteries of Progress: Infrastructure Development

A robust infrastructure network is the lifeblood of any thriving economy. Singapore recognized this and prioritized the development of:

- **Transportation**: A world-class transportation system was established, including efficient public transportation networks, a modern airport, and a well-maintained road network. This not only facilitated the movement of goods and people but also fostered a vibrant trade environment.
- **Communication**: Investments were made in state-of-the-art communication infrastructure, ensuring seamless connectivity both domestically and internationally. This attracted foreign investors who

needed reliable communication channels and fostered collaboration within the growing economy.

- **Energy and Utilities**: Reliable and efficient energy and utilities infrastructure provided a stable foundation for businesses to operate. This included investments in power generation, water treatment, and waste management systems.

By building a robust infrastructure network, Singapore created an environment conducive to business growth and innovation.

Creating a Haven for Businesses: A Business-Friendly Environment

Singapore meticulously crafted a business environment that was attractive to foreign investors. Here's how they achieved this:

- **Stable and Predictable Policies**: The government established a stable political environment with clear and consistent economic policies. This predictability allowed businesses to plan for the future with confidence, fostering long-term investment.

- **Favorable Tax Regime**: A competitive tax regime was implemented, offering tax breaks and incentives for businesses to establish and grow their operations in Singapore. This strategy not only attracted foreign investment but also encouraged local entrepreneurship.

- **Reduced Bureaucracy**: The government streamlined bureaucratic processes, making it easier for businesses to obtain permits and navigate regulations. This minimized red tape and allowed companies to focus on their core activities.

- **Skilled Workforce**: As discussed earlier, Singapore's focus on education ensured a readily available pool of skilled and educated workers. This eliminated the need for companies to invest heavily in training programs themselves, making them more competitive in the global market.

By creating a business-friendly environment, Singapore positioned itself as a magnet for foreign investment. This influx of capital fueled rapid economic growth and job creation, propelling the nation towards prosperity.

The Singaporean Synergy: A Foundation for Success

It's important to note that these three pillars – education, infrastructure, and a business-friendly environment – didn't exist in isolation. They functioned in a synergistic manner, each element reinforcing the others. A well-educated workforce attracted businesses, which in turn, created demand for more skilled workers. Robust infrastructure facilitated trade and business activities, further fueling economic growth and the need for continued investment in education. This virtuous cycle propelled Singapore's remarkable transformation.

Learning from the Lion City: Applying Singapore's Strategies

While replicating Singapore's exact model may not be feasible for every nation, the underlying principles are universally applicable. By prioritizing education and infrastructure development, and by creating an environment that welcomes and supports businesses, any country can create a solid foundation for sustainable economic growth and prosperity.

In the next chapter, we'll delve deeper into Singapore's journey, exploring how they transitioned from a manufacturing base to a knowledge economy and how they adapted their workforce development strategies to meet the demands of the 21st century.

Chapter 3: The Skills Revolution - How Singapore shifted from a manufacturing base to a knowledge economy and the corresponding workforce development strategies.

Singapore's economic story isn't a linear one. It's a captivating tale of continuous adaptation and evolution. Having established a strong foundation through education, infrastructure, and a business-friendly environment, Singapore embarked on its next challenge: transitioning from a labor-intensive manufacturing base to a knowledge-driven economy.

The Winds of Change: Why the Shift Became Necessary

The global economic landscape was undergoing a significant transformation. Manufacturing jobs were increasingly moving to countries with lower labor costs. Singapore, with its limited land and natural resources, recognized the need to diversify its economy and move up the value chain.

The Knowledge Economy Beckons

The knowledge economy thrives on innovation, research and development, and a highly skilled workforce. Singapore set its sights on becoming a global hub for these activities. Here's how they navigated this shift:

- **Investing in R&D**: The government poured resources into research and development initiatives, establishing world-class research institutions and universities specializing in cutting-edge fields like biotechnology, information technology, and engineering.
- **Attracting Talent**: Singapore actively sought to attract top international talent by offering competitive salaries, research grants, and a vibrant working environment.
- **Nurturing Innovation**: A culture of innovation was fostered by encouraging entrepreneurship, providing seed funding for startups, and establishing innovation

centers to facilitate collaboration between researchers, businesses, and investors.

Upskilling and Reskilling the Workforce

This shift towards a knowledge economy demanded a corresponding upgrade in the skillset of the workforce. Here's how Singapore tackled this challenge:

- **Lifelong Learning on Steroids**: The existing focus on lifelong learning was intensified. Training programs were tailored to equip workers with the skills needed for the knowledge economy, including digital literacy, critical thinking, problem-solving, and the ability to collaborate effectively in a globalized environment.
- **Industry-Specific Partnerships**: The government partnered with key industries to identify specific skill gaps and develop targeted training programs. This ensured the workforce possessed the skills most desired by employers.

- **Focus on Soft Skills**: In addition to technical skills, Singapore recognized the importance of soft skills such as communication, teamwork, and adaptability. Training programs were designed to cultivate these qualities, fostering a workforce that could thrive in a rapidly evolving environment.

Case Study: The Biopolis Transformation

A prime example of Singapore's successful skills revolution is the Biopolis initiative. This purpose-built life sciences hub houses research institutions, biotechnology companies, and academic institutions. The government actively partnered with industry leaders to identify the specific skills needed for this sector. Training programs were developed, and targeted incentives were offered to attract and retain talent. Today, Biopolis is a thriving hub for biomedical research, attracting global players and contributing significantly to Singapore's knowledge economy.

The Ever-Evolving Journey

Singapore's commitment to workforce development isn't a one-time accomplishment; it's an ongoing process. As technology continues to advance and the global economy undergoes further transformations, Singapore is constantly adapting its strategies. Here are some ongoing initiatives:

- **Embracing Automation**: Singapore recognizes that automation will play a significant role in the future of work. They are preparing their workforce by equipping them with the skills to manage and work alongside intelligent machines.
- **Focus on Artificial Intelligence**: Training programs are being developed to equip workers with the skills needed to develop, implement, and manage artificial intelligence technologies.
- **Fostering a Culture of Entrepreneurship**: Entrepreneurship is seen as a key driver of innovation and economic growth. Programs are being implemented to encourage individuals to develop their

entrepreneurial skills and launch their own businesses.

Lessons from the Lion City: Adapting Your Workforce Strategies

Singapore's experience offers valuable lessons for organizations worldwide. As technology continues to disrupt industries and reshape the world of work, the ability to adapt your workforce development strategies is paramount. Here are some key takeaways:

- **Embrace Lifelong Learning**: Make continuous learning a core value within your organization. Encourage your employees to upskill and reskill themselves to remain relevant in the evolving job market.
- **Partner with Industry Leaders**: Collaborate with industry experts to identify the specific skill sets needed for your sector. Develop targeted training programs based on this industry-specific knowledge.

- **Focus on Soft Skills**: While technical skills are crucial, don't neglect the importance of soft skills. Invest in programs that nurture communication, teamwork, and adaptability within your workforce.
- **Foster a Culture of Innovation**: Create an environment that encourages creativity and critical thinking. Empower your employees to experiment and develop innovative solutions.

By adopting these strategies, you can prepare your workforce for the future, ensuring your organization remains competitive and thrives in the ever-changing economic landscape.

Chapter 4: The Singapore Advantage - Key takeaways from Singapore's approach - focus on lifelong learning, meritocracy, and building a strong government-industry partnership.

Lifelong Learning: A Cornerstone of Adaptability

Singapore recognized that education wasn't a one-time event; it's a lifelong journey. Here's how they fostered a culture of continuous learning:

- **Emphasis on Skills, Not Just Degrees**: The education system focused on equipping individuals with not just theoretical knowledge but also practical skills applicable to the workplace. This focus on lifelong learning ensured their workforce remained adaptable and relevant in the face of rapid technological advancements.
- **Readily Available Training Programs**: A vast network of training programs was established, catering to diverse needs and career stages. This

allowed individuals to continuously upgrade their skills throughout their careers.

- **Government Support for Lifelong Learning**: The government actively encouraged and subsidized participation in training programs. This financial assistance made lifelong learning more accessible and encouraged individuals to invest in their own development.

Meritocracy: Rewarding Talent and Hard Work

Singapore's meritocratic system played a crucial role in attracting and retaining top talent. Here's how it functioned:

- **Focus on Performance**: The system rewarded individuals based on their skills, performance, and contributions. This meritocratic approach motivated individuals to excel and strive for continuous improvement.

- **Equal Opportunities for All**: While meritocracy emphasizes performance, Singapore's system aimed to ensure equal opportunities for all. This was achieved through accessible education and a focus on identifying and nurturing talent regardless of background.
- **Attracting Top Talent**: A meritocratic system fostered a competitive environment that attracted high-performing individuals from within Singapore and abroad. This influx of talent further fueled innovation and economic growth.

Government-Industry Partnership: A Collaborative Force

Singapore's success story wouldn't be complete without acknowledging the strong partnership between the government and the private sector. Let's explore its key aspects:

- **Joint Skill Gap Identification**: The government and industry leaders worked together to identify specific skill gaps within the workforce. This ensured training programs were tailored to meet the actual needs of businesses.
- **Developing Targeted Training Programs**: Based on the identified skill gaps, collaborative efforts were undertaken to develop targeted training programs that equipped workers with the specific skills demanded by the evolving job market.
- **Shared Investment**: The government and private sector often shared the costs of training programs, making them more accessible to businesses and individuals.

The Synergy of the Singapore Advantage

These three elements – lifelong learning, meritocracy, and a strong government-industry partnership – functioned in a synergistic manner. A culture of continuous learning facilitated the development of a highly skilled workforce.

Meritocracy ensured that the most talented individuals were identified and nurtured. And the government-industry partnership helped identify skills gaps and develop targeted training programs that met the needs of both businesses and workers. This virtuous cycle propelled Singapore's economic success.

The Singapore Advantage: Takeaways for Your Organization

While replicating the Singaporean model in its entirety might not be feasible for every organization, the underlying principles hold valuable lessons:

- **Invest in Lifelong Learning**: Foster a culture of continuous learning within your organization. Encourage employees to take advantage of training programs and professional development opportunities.

- **Embrace Meritocracy**: Create a system that rewards performance and hard work. Recognize and celebrate the achievements of your top performers.
- **Build Partnerships**: Collaborate with industry experts and educational institutions to identify skill gaps and develop relevant training programs for your workforce.

Chapter 5: Assessing Your Workforce Needs - Identifying skill gaps, understanding future trends, and setting goals for workforce development.

The journey to unleashing Workforce Mojo within your organization begins with a clear understanding of your current state. This chapter will equip you with the tools and strategies to conduct a comprehensive needs assessment, allowing you to identify skill gaps, anticipate future trends, and set achievable goals for your workforce development initiatives.

Taking Stock: A Skills Gap Analysis

The first step is to gain a clear picture of the skills your workforce currently possesses and compare it to the skills you'll need to achieve your strategic goals. Here's how to conduct a thorough skills gap analysis:

- **Job Descriptions and Skill Inventories**: Reviewing job descriptions and conducting skills inventories through surveys or assessments will reveal the specific technical and soft skills required for each role within your organization.
- **Performance Reviews and Feedback**: Analyze performance reviews and employee feedback to identify areas where skill development is needed. Look for trends in performance gaps or areas where employees consistently struggle.
- **Managerial Input**: Seek insights from managers who have a firsthand understanding of their team's strengths and weaknesses.

Future-Proofing Your Workforce: Understanding Industry Trends

The world of work is in constant flux. To ensure your workforce remains relevant, it's crucial to anticipate future trends. Here are some ways to stay ahead of the curve:

- **Industry Reports and Publications**: Stay updated on industry reports and publications that forecast future skills demands within your sector.
- **Conferences and Events**: Participating in industry conferences and events allows you to network with experts and gain insights into emerging trends.
- **Competitor Analysis**: Analyze how your competitors are approaching workforce development. This can provide valuable insights into the skills they believe will be crucial for future success.

By combining internal assessment data with external trend analysis, you'll gain a comprehensive understanding of the evolving skill landscape. This allows you to identify potential skill gaps and prioritize the development areas that will be most impactful for your organization's future success.

Setting SMART Goals for Workforce Development

Once you've identified skill gaps and anticipated future trends, it's time to set goals for your workforce development initiatives. Remember, effective goals should be SMART – Specific, Measurable, Achievable, Relevant, and Time-bound.

- **Specific**: Instead of a vague goal like "improve communication skills," define a specific skill like "active listening" or "effective presentation skills."
- **Measurable**: Quantify your goals whenever possible. This could be a percentage of employees completing a training program or a measurable improvement in a performance metric.

- **Achievable**: Set goals that are ambitious yet attainable. Unrealistic goals can lead to discouragement and a lack of motivation.
- **Relevant**: Ensure your goals are aligned with your overall business strategy and contribute to the achievement of your organizational objectives.
- **Time-bound**: Set a specific timeframe for achieving your goals. This creates a sense of urgency and facilitates progress tracking.

Building Your Workforce Development Roadmap

With your needs assessment complete and SMART goals established, you're ready to create a roadmap for developing your workforce. This roadmap will outline the specific strategies and initiatives you'll implement to bridge skill gaps and cultivate a culture of ongoing learning.

Chapter 6: Building a Culture of Learning - Creating a Supportive Environment that Encourages Continuous Learning and Development

In today's rapidly changing world, fostering a culture of continuous learning is no longer a luxury, it's a necessity. This chapter looks into the key principles and practices that can transform your environment into a breeding ground for personal and professional growth.

Why is a Culture of Learning Important?

A culture of learning offers a multitude of benefits for both individuals and organizations:

- **Enhanced Innovation and Problem-Solving:** Employees equipped with the latest knowledge and skills can approach challenges with fresh perspectives and develop creative solutions.

- **Improved Adaptability:** In a dynamic environment, the ability to learn and adapt is crucial. A culture of learning fosters a growth mindset, encouraging employees to embrace change and new skills.
- **Increased Employee Engagement:** When employees feel supported in their development, they become more invested in their work and the organization's success.
- **Attracting and Retaining Top Talent:** A strong learning culture is a magnet for talented individuals seeking opportunities for continual growth.

Building the Foundation: Key Components

Here are some essential elements for building a supportive learning culture:

- **Leadership that Champions Learning:** Leaders set the tone. When leaders themselves demonstrate a commitment to learning and development, it sends a powerful message to the whole organization.

- **Learning Mindset:** Cultivate a growth mindset where mistakes are seen as learning opportunities and effort is valued over innate talent.
- **Open Communication:** Encourage open communication and knowledge sharing. This can be done through forums, mentorship programs, or brown bag lunches where colleagues share their expertise.
- **Access to Learning Resources:** Provide employees with access to a variety of learning resources, including online courses, workshops, conferences, and professional development books.

Making Learning Engaging and Rewarding

Learning shouldn't feel like a chore. Here are some ways to make the process engaging and rewarding:

- **Variety in Learning Methods:** Offer a diverse range of learning methods to cater to different learning styles. This can include online modules, hands-on workshops, or even gamified learning experiences.

- **Social Learning:** Encourage collaboration and peer-to-peer learning. This can be facilitated through group projects, team discussions, or online learning communities.
- **Recognition and Appreciation:** Celebrate learning achievements! Recognize and reward employees who actively participate in learning and development initiatives.

Conclusion

Building a culture of learning is an ongoing process. By implementing these strategies and fostering a supportive environment, you can empower your employees to become lifelong learners, driving innovation, growth, and success for your organization.

This chapter serves as a springboard for further exploration. Consider these additional questions:

- What are some specific challenges your organization faces in fostering a culture of learning?

- How can you tailor your learning and development programs to address the unique needs of your employees?
- What metrics can you use to track the progress and impact of your learning culture initiatives?

By addressing these questions and taking continuous action, you can cultivate a thriving learning culture that fuels individual and organizational excellence.

Chapter 7: Investing in Training and Development Programs - Tailoring programs to address specific skill needs and career aspirations.

Chapter 6 focused on building a culture of learning, the foundation for employee growth. Now, let's delve deeper into the strategic development of training and development programs. This chapter explores how to tailor programs to address the specific skill needs and career aspirations of your workforce.

Identifying Skill Gaps

Effective training starts with a clear understanding of the skills your employees need to succeed. Here are some methods for needs identification:

- **Performance Appraisals:** Analyze performance reviews to identify areas where employees might need additional development.

- **Skills Gap Analysis:** Compare the skills your employees currently possess with the skills required for their current and future roles.
- **Task Analysis:** Break down specific jobs into their component tasks and identify the necessary skills for each task.
- **Employee Surveys and Feedback:** Solicit input directly from employees about their learning needs and career aspirations.

Tailoring Programs for Individual Growth

A one-size-fits-all approach to training rarely yields optimal results. Here's how to create targeted programs:

- **Individual Development Plans (IDPs):** Work with each employee to create a personalized IDP outlining their desired skill development and aligning it with organizational goals.

- **Multi-Level Training:** Offer programs at varying levels of difficulty to cater to different experience levels and knowledge bases.
- **Mentorship and Coaching Programs:** Pair experienced employees with newer colleagues to provide personalized guidance and support skill development.

Bridging the Gap Between Training and Application

The true value of training lies in its application. Here are some strategies to bridge the gap:

- **On-the-Job Learning:** Provide opportunities for employees to apply newly acquired skills in their daily work.
- **Post-Training Support:** Offer ongoing support through coaching, mentoring, or access to resources to help employees solidify their learnings.

- **Performance Measurement:** Track the impact of training programs by measuring changes in employee performance or achievement of specific goals.

Investing in Career Development

Training shouldn't be limited to immediate skill needs. Consider these strategies to support career aspirations:

- **Career Pathing:** Outline potential career paths within the organization and the skills required at each stage.
- **Leadership Development Programs:** Invest in programs that equip high-potential employees with the necessary skills for leadership roles.
- **Tuition Reimbursement:** Offer financial assistance for employees pursuing educational opportunities relevant to their career goals.

Conclusion

By tailoring training and development programs to address specific skill needs and career aspirations, you create a win-win situation. Employees gain valuable knowledge and skills, while organizations benefit from a more engaged, adaptable, and future-proof workforce.

This chapter provides a framework for developing targeted programs. Remember, effective training is an ongoing process. Regularly evaluate your programs, gather feedback, and adapt them to meet the evolving needs of your employees and organization.

Chapter 8: Fostering Engagement and Motivation - Strategies to keep employees engaged, motivated, and satisfied in their roles.

Employee engagement and motivation are crucial for organizational success. Engaged employees are more productive, innovative, and less likely to leave the company. This chapter explores strategies to cultivate a work environment that fosters these qualities.

Understanding Engagement and Motivation

Employee engagement goes beyond just satisfaction. It's a deep-seated commitment to the organization's goals and values. Motivation is the driving force that compels employees to exert effort and achieve their full potential.

Factors Affecting Engagement and Motivation

Several factors influence employee engagement and motivation, including:

- **Meaningful Work:** Employees crave work that they find purposeful and contributes to a larger goal.
- **Recognition and Appreciation:** Feeling valued and appreciated for their contributions is a powerful motivator.
- **Growth Opportunities:** Employees want opportunities to learn, develop new skills, and advance their careers.
- **Work-Life Balance:** A healthy work-life balance helps employees avoid burnout and maintain long-term motivation.
- **Positive Work Environment:** A supportive and collaborative work environment fosters a sense of belonging and well-being.

Strategies to Foster Engagement and Motivation

Here are some practical strategies to cultivate a more engaged and motivated workforce:

- **Empowerment and Autonomy:** Give employees ownership over their work and the freedom to make decisions.
- **Clear Goals and Expectations:** Ensure employees understand their roles, responsibilities, and how their work contributes to the organization's goals.
- **Regular Feedback and Coaching:** Provide ongoing feedback to help employees understand their strengths and areas for improvement.
- **Open Communication:** Foster a culture of open communication where employees feel comfortable sharing ideas and concerns.
- **Recognition and Rewards:** Recognize and reward employees for their achievements, both big and small.

This can include public recognition, bonuses, or additional development opportunities.

- **Promote Work-Life Balance:** Offer flexible work arrangements, generous vacation time, and resources to help employees manage their personal lives.
- **Invest in Employee Wellbeing:** Promote employee well-being by offering health and wellness programs, creating a healthy work environment, and addressing issues like stress and burnout.
- **Team Building Activities:** Organize team-building activities to foster collaboration, communication, and a sense of community.

The Power of Recognition

Recognition is a powerful tool for boosting motivation and engagement. Here are some effective ways to recognize employees:

- **Public Recognition:** Acknowledge achievements during team meetings, company newsletters, or social media.
- **Peer-to-Peer Recognition:** Encourage employees to recognize and appreciate each other's contributions.
- **Personalized Rewards:** Tailor rewards to individual preferences, such as additional time off, professional development opportunities, or tickets to events.

Conclusion

Fostering engagement and motivation is an ongoing process. By implementing these strategies and creating a positive work environment, you can empower your employees to reach their full potential and drive organizational success. Remember, the most effective strategies will consider the unique needs and preferences of your workforce.

This chapter provides a starting point. As you move forward, consider the following:

- How can you measure employee engagement and motivation within your organization?
- What are some creative ways to recognize and reward employees in your specific workplace culture?
- How can you tailor your strategies to address the diverse needs of your workforce?

By dedicating time and effort to fostering engagement and motivation, you can cultivate a thriving work environment where employees feel valued, empowered, and excited to contribute.

Chapter 9: Measuring Success - Tracking the Impact of Your Workforce Development Initiatives and Making Adjustments As Needed

Investing in workforce development is crucial, but its true value lies in its impact on your organization. This chapter explores strategies for measuring the success of your initiatives and making adjustments to ensure they continue to meet your evolving needs.

Why Measure Success?

Measuring success serves several important purposes:

- **Demonstrates ROI (Return on Investment):** Quantify the return you're getting on your investment in workforce development programs.
- **Identifies Areas for Improvement:** Data can reveal areas where your programs are falling short and pinpoint opportunities for improvement.

- **Informs Future Decisions:** Data-driven insights can guide future program development and resource allocation.
- **Boosts Accountability:** Tracking progress keeps everyone accountable for achieving workforce development goals.

Metrics for Measuring Success

The specific metrics you choose will depend on the nature of your programs and organizational goals. Here's a framework to get you started:

1. Learning and Development Outcomes:

- **Training Completion Rates:** Track the percentage of employees who complete assigned training programs.
- **Knowledge and Skill Assessments:** Measure the increase in knowledge and skills acquired through training programs.

- **Learner Satisfaction:** Gather feedback from employees to gauge their satisfaction with training programs.

2. Business Impact Outcomes:

- **Employee Engagement and Retention Rates:** Track changes in employee engagement and retention after implementing workforce development initiatives.
- **Performance Improvement:** Measure improvements in employee performance, such as increased productivity or quality of work.
- **Innovation:** Track the number of new ideas, inventions, or process improvements generated by employees.

3. Cost-Benefit Analysis:

- **Cost per Employee:** Calculate the total cost of a program divided by the number of employees who participated.

- **Return on Investment (ROI):** Measure the financial benefits of your programs compared to the costs of development and implementation.

Data Collection Methods

There are various methods for collecting data to measure success, including:

- **Learning Management Systems (LMS) Reports:** Many LMS platforms provide reports on training completion rates and learner activity.
- **Surveys and Feedback Forms:** Conduct surveys and feedback forms to gather employee input on training programs and overall work environment.
- **Performance Management Data:** Analyze data from performance reviews to track changes in employee performance.
- **Financial Data:** Track costs associated with program development and implementation, as well as any measurable financial benefits.

Making Adjustments and Continuous Improvement

Measurement is valuable only if it leads to action. Here's how to use data to improve your programs:

- **Analyze Results:** Regularly analyze data to identify trends and areas for improvement.
- **Make Adjustments:** Based on your analysis, adapt your programs to address identified shortcomings or capitalize on successful elements.
- **Communicate and Share Results:** Communicate the impact of your workforce development initiatives to stakeholders to build support and demonstrate the value of these programs.

Conclusion

Measuring the success of your workforce development initiatives is an essential step in ensuring they deliver the desired results. By tracking progress, gathering data, and making adjustments as needed, you can continuously improve your programs, empower your workforce, and drive long-term organizational success.

This chapter provides a foundation for measuring success. Remember, the most effective metrics will be aligned with your specific goals and organizational context. As you move forward, consider the following:

- What are the key performance indicators (KPIs) that matter most to your organization?
- How can you ensure data collection is efficient and doesn't overburden employees?
- How can you establish a culture of continuous improvement within your workforce development initiatives?

By embracing a data-driven approach and a commitment to ongoing improvement, you can ensure your workforce development efforts yield a significant return on your investment.

Chapter 10: Companies That Get It Right - Showcase real-world examples of organizations that have successfully invested in their workforce and achieved significant results.

Singapore's economic strength is undeniably linked to its highly skilled workforce. This chapter showcases how prominent Singaporean companies are reaping significant rewards by investing in their employees' development.

1. Singapore Airlines: Soaring High with a Skilled Workforce

(Industry: Aviation)

Singapore Airlines (SIA) exemplifies excellence in the aviation industry. Their reputation rests heavily on the quality of service delivered by their employees. Here's how SIA prioritizes workforce development:

- **Singapore Airlines Academy:** This world-renowned institution offers a comprehensive training program for pilots, cabin crew, and other aviation professionals. The curriculum emphasizes not only technical expertise but also service excellence and cultural awareness. This holistic approach ensures passengers receive an exceptional travel experience, consistently placing SIA at the top of customer satisfaction surveys.

- **Skills Future Programs:** SIA actively collaborates with government initiatives like Skills Future. These programs equip employees with the skills needed for the evolving aviation landscape, encompassing advanced aircraft technology, data analytics, and cybersecurity. By embracing continuous learning, SIA ensures its workforce remains future-proof.
- **Leadership Development Programs:** Recognizing the importance of strong leadership across all levels, SIA offers targeted programs to nurture future leaders. These programs empower individuals to navigate the complexities of the aviation industry, ensuring a pipeline of skilled leaders for continued success.

SIA's commitment to its people is evident in their highly skilled and service-oriented workforce. This investment in talent development is a key factor in their position as a global leader in aviation.

2. Singapore Economic Development Board (EDB): Cultivating a Culture of Innovation

(Industry: Government Agency)

The Singapore Economic Development Board (EDB) plays a pivotal role in attracting and developing talent for Singapore's growing economy. They actively promote a culture of innovation through various initiatives:

- **Global Ready Talent Pool:** The EDB fosters a talent pool equipped to handle the demands of a globalized economy. This includes programs to attract international talent with specialized skills, while also upskilling the domestic workforce to meet industry needs.

- **Industry Collaboration:** Recognizing the importance of industry-specific expertise, the EDB collaborates with companies to develop customized training programs. This ensures employees are equipped with the skills most relevant to their specific industry and roles.
- **Focus on STEM Education:** The EDB actively supports initiatives that promote Science, Technology, Engineering, and Math (STEM) education at all levels. This focus on building a strong foundation in STEM fields ensures a future pipeline of talent for Singapore's innovation-driven economy.

The EDB's commitment to workforce development fosters a dynamic and adaptable workforce. This, in turn, fuels Singapore's position as a global hub for innovation and attracts leading companies to establish their base in the country.

3. DBS Bank: Building a Future-Ready Workforce

(Industry: Banking & Finance)

DBS Bank, a leading financial institution in Southeast Asia, recognizes the need for a future-ready workforce in the rapidly evolving banking landscape. Here's how they invest in their employees:

- **DBS Academy:** This in-house learning and development arm offers a comprehensive range of programs, from technical skills training to leadership development workshops. The focus is on equipping employees with the skills needed to thrive in the digital age, including data analytics, artificial intelligence, and cybersecurity.
- **Learning Culture:** DBS fosters a culture of continuous learning by encouraging employees to take ownership of their development. They offer flexible learning options, including online courses,

mentorship programs, and opportunities to participate in industry conferences.

- **Career Development Programs:** DBS recognizes the importance of career growth. They provide career development programs that help employees identify their strengths and aspirations, and map out a personalized career path within the organization.

By investing in their people, DBS empowers its workforce to adapt to the changing financial landscape. This commitment to continuous learning has positioned them as a leader in digital banking and innovation within the region.

Conclusion

These Singaporean companies serve as prime examples of how investing in workforce development can lead to significant success. Their commitment to fostering a skilled, adaptable, and future-oriented workforce is a key driver of Singapore's economic growth and global competitiveness. By following their lead, other organizations can cultivate a thriving workforce that drives innovation and achieves long-term success.

Chapter 11: Challenges and Opportunities - Navigating the Roadblocks to Workforce Development Success

Building a strong workforce development strategy is an investment in your organization's future. However, the road to success is rarely smooth. This chapter explores the potential challenges you might encounter and equips you with strategies to overcome them.

Challenge #1: Securing Leadership Buy-In

- **Symptoms:** Leaders view workforce development as a cost center, not a strategic investment. Limited resources are allocated, and programs lack strong leadership support.
- **Solutions:**
    - **Demonstrate ROI:** Quantify the potential return on investment (ROI) of workforce development initiatives. Present data on how improved skills

can lead to increased productivity, reduced turnover, and enhanced innovation.
- **Focus on Business Goals:** Align workforce development initiatives with the organization's overall strategic goals. Highlight how these programs can help achieve specific business objectives, such as entering new markets or launching new product lines.
- **Get Executive Sponsors:** Identify passionate leaders within the organization who can champion workforce development initiatives. Their support can be instrumental in securing resources and driving program adoption.

Challenge #2: Identifying Skill Gaps

- **Symptoms:** Organizations lack a clear understanding of the skills currently possessed by their workforce and the skills needed for future success. Training programs may not address the most critical skill gaps.
- **Solutions:**

- **Conduct Skills Gap Analysis:** Use a systematic approach to identify the skills needed for each role within the organization. Compare this to the existing skill sets of your employees. This will reveal areas where development is necessary.
- **Employee Surveys and Feedback:** Gather input directly from employees through surveys and focus groups. This can provide valuable insights into their perceived skill gaps and development needs.
- **Performance Management Data:** Analyze data from performance reviews and evaluations. This can reveal areas where employees are consistently struggling, indicating potential skill gaps.

Challenge #3: Designing Effective Training Programs

- **Symptoms:** Training programs are generic and one-size-fits-all, failing to cater to different learning styles and employee needs. The content may not be relevant to employees' actual job functions, leading to low engagement and limited learning transfer.

- **Solutions:**
  - **Needs-Based Design:** Develop training programs based on the specific skill gaps identified through your analysis. Ensure the content is relevant to employees' roles and responsibilities.
  - **Variety in Learning Methods:** Offer a diverse range of learning methods to cater to different learning styles. This can include online courses, instructor-led workshops, hands-on simulations, or even gamified learning experiences.
  - **Microlearning:** Break down complex topics into smaller, bite-sized modules that are easy to digest and implement in busy schedules.
  - **Involve Subject Matter Experts:** Tap into the expertise of your employees by involving them in the design and delivery of training programs.

Challenge #4: Ensuring Transfer of Learning

- **Symptoms:** Employees attend training programs but struggle to apply the newly acquired skills in their daily work. The learning doesn't translate into improved performance or behavior change.
- **Solutions:**
    - **On-the-Job Application:** Provide opportunities for employees to practice their new skills immediately after training. This could involve role-playing exercises, mentoring programs, or pilot projects where they can apply their learnings in a safe environment.
    - **Post-Training Support:** Offer ongoing support to employees after completing a training program. This could include coaching sessions, access to resources, or knowledge-sharing forums to help them solidify their understanding and overcome challenges during application.

- **Performance Management Integration:** Integrate learning objectives into performance management systems. This reinforces the importance of skill development and holds employees accountable for applying their new skills.

Challenge #5: Measuring the Impact of Training

- **Symptoms:** Organizations struggle to measure the effectiveness of their workforce development initiatives. The true impact on employee performance, business outcomes, or ROI remains unclear.
- **Solutions:**
  - **Define Success Metrics:** Determine what success looks like for your workforce development programs. This could involve metrics related to learner engagement, knowledge gain, skill application, improved performance, or increased productivity.

- **Collect Data:** Utilize various data collection methods to track progress and measure impact. This could include pre- and post-training assessments, surveys, performance data, or customer satisfaction ratings.
- **Regular Evaluation:** Regularly evaluate the effectiveness of your training programs based on the data collected. This allows you to identify areas for improvement and adapt your programs for continued success.

Challenge #6: Budgetary Constraints

- **Symptoms:** Limited resources hinder the development and implementation of comprehensive workforce development programs. Organizations may struggle to afford high-quality training materials or instructor-led workshops.

- **Solutions:**
    - **Cost-Effective Training Methods:** Explore cost-effective training methods that deliver high value. This could include online learning platforms with subscription models, leveraging internal expertise for knowledge sharing, or partnering with industry associations for discounted training programs.
    - **Focus on High-Impact Initiatives:** Prioritize initiatives that offer the greatest return on investment. Conduct a cost-benefit analysis to identify programs that will have the most significant impact on employee performance and business outcomes.
    - **Seek Funding:** Explore external funding opportunities for workforce development programs. This could involve government grants, industry partnerships, or collaborating with educational institutions.

Challenge #7: Lack of Time and Capacity

- **Symptoms:** Employees are already stretched thin and lack the time to participate in training programs. Managers may feel overwhelmed by the additional responsibility of overseeing employee development.
- **Solutions:**
    - **Microlearning and Blended Learning:** Offer bite-sized learning modules and blended learning approaches that combine online and offline components. This allows employees to learn at their own pace and in short bursts that can be easily integrated into their busy schedules.
    - **Mobile Learning:** Utilize mobile learning platforms to deliver training content that can be accessed on-demand from any device. This provides employees with the flexibility to learn during commutes, breaks, or whenever they have a few spare minutes.
    - **Manager Development:** Equip managers with the skills and resources to support employee

development. Provide training on coaching, mentoring, and performance management techniques. Empower them to create a culture of learning within their teams.

Challenge #8: Resistance to Change

- **Symptoms:** Employees may be resistant to change and new learning initiatives. They may feel comfortable with their current skill sets and see training as a disruption to their daily workflow.
- **Solutions:**
  - **Communication and Transparency:** Communicate the rationale behind workforce development initiatives clearly and transparently. Explain how these programs will benefit both employees and the organization.
  - **Employee Involvement:** Involve employees in the planning and design of training programs. This can help build buy-in and ownership over their development journey.

- **Focus on Benefits:** Highlight the benefits of continuous learning for employees. This could include opportunities for career advancement, increased earning potential, or enhanced job security.

Challenge #9: Measuring Long-Term Impact

- **Symptoms:** Organizations struggle to measure the long-term impact of workforce development initiatives on employee engagement, retention, and innovation.
- **Solutions:**
  - **Longitudinal Studies:** Conduct longitudinal studies to track the impact of training programs over time. This can involve measuring changes in employee engagement, retention rates, innovation output, or customer satisfaction metrics.
  - **Balanced Scorecard Approach:** Utilize a balanced scorecard approach that considers both short-term and long-term impacts of workforce

development initiatives. This will provide a more holistic view of the program's value.
- **Focus on Leading Indicators:** Track leading indicators that can predict future outcomes. For example, measure employee participation in learning activities, knowledge retention rates, or manager satisfaction with the program's effectiveness.

Challenge #10: Aligning Development with Career Paths

- **Symptoms:** Training programs may not be aligned with individual career aspirations. Employees may not see a clear connection between their development and future opportunities within the organization.
- **Solutions:**
  - **Individual Development Plans (IDPs):** Develop personalized IDPs with each employee. These plans should outline their career goals and

identify the skill development needed to achieve them.

- **Mentorship and Coaching Programs:** Implement mentorship and coaching programs that connect employees with experienced professionals who can guide their career development.
- **Internal Job Boards:** Promote internal job boards and career development opportunities within the organization. This demonstrates your commitment to employee growth and helps employees see a future for themselves within the company.

Conclusion

Building a strong workforce development strategy is an ongoing process. By acknowledging potential challenges and implementing these solutions, you can overcome these roadblocks and create a thriving learning environment. Remember, the most successful organizations are those that prioritize continuous learning and invest in the development of their greatest asset: their people.

Chapter 12: The Future of Work - Embracing Emerging Trends in Workforce Development

The future of work is constantly evolving, driven by technological advancements, globalization, and demographic shifts. This chapter explores key trends that will shape workforce development in the years to come and provides guidance on how to prepare your organization for success in this dynamic landscape.

Emerging Trends in Workforce Development

- **Focus on Lifelong Learning:** The rapid pace of change necessitates a shift towards lifelong learning. Employees will need to continuously develop new skills and adapt to evolving technologies throughout their careers. Organizations will need to provide ongoing learning opportunities and encourage a culture of continuous self-improvement.

- **Rise of Automation and AI:** Automation and Artificial Intelligence (AI) will increasingly automate routine tasks. While some jobs will be displaced, new opportunities will emerge. The focus will shift towards developing skills that complement AI, such as critical thinking, creativity, problem-solving, and complex communication.
- **In-Demand Skills:** The demand for skills in areas like data analytics, cybersecurity, cloud computing, and digital marketing will continue to grow. Organizations will need to invest in developing these skills within their workforce or attract talent with these capabilities.
- **The Gig Economy and Remote Work:** The gig economy and remote work arrangements are becoming increasingly prevalent. Organizations will need to develop flexible learning and development solutions that cater to a more dispersed workforce.
- **Focus on Soft Skills:** Soft skills, such as communication, collaboration, teamwork, and adaptability, will become even more crucial for success in the future workplace. These skills are

essential for navigating complex projects, fostering innovation, and building strong relationships in a dynamic work environment.

- **Personalization and Microlearning:** Learning and development will become more personalized and bite-sized. Microlearning approaches, delivered through mobile platforms and online modules, will enable employees to learn at their own pace and in short bursts that fit their busy schedules.
- **Focus on Wellbeing:** Organizations will increasingly recognize the importance of employee wellbeing in a climate of constant change and skill development. This may involve offering programs on stress management, mindfulness, and work-life balance, fostering a healthy and productive work environment.

Preparing Your Organization for the Future of Work

Here's how you can prepare your organization for the future of work:

- **Conduct a Skills Gap Analysis:** Regularly assess your current workforce skills and identify any gaps compared to future needs. This will inform your workforce development strategy and ensure you're developing the right skills for success.
- **Invest in Learning Technologies:** Leverage technology to create engaging and accessible learning experiences. Explore platforms like Learning Management Systems (LMS), virtual reality (VR), augmented reality (AR), and Artificial Intelligence (AI) to personalize learning and make development more immersive.
- **Develop a Culture of Learning:** Foster a culture where continuous learning is valued and encouraged.

Create opportunities for knowledge sharing, peer-to-peer learning, and collaboration. Recognize and reward employees who demonstrate a growth mindset and actively participate in learning initiatives.

- **Build Partnerships:** Partner with educational institutions and industry associations to access the latest learning resources and expertise. Explore opportunities for co-creating customized training programs that align with your specific needs.

- **Promote Agility and Adaptability:** Develop a culture of agility and adaptability within your organization. Encourage employees to embrace change, experiment with new ideas, and continuously seek feedback and improvement.

- **Prioritize Employee Wellbeing:** Recognize the importance of employee wellbeing. Offer programs and resources that support mental and physical health, promote work-life balance, and create a positive and supportive work environment.

- **Embrace Diversity and Inclusion:** Diversity and inclusion are essential for fostering innovation and attracting top talent. Develop programs that promote inclusivity and create a workplace where everyone feels valued and empowered to contribute their unique skills and perspectives.

Conclusion

The future of work presents both challenges and opportunities. By embracing emerging trends in workforce development and taking proactive steps to prepare your organization, you can ensure your workforce has the skills and agility needed to thrive in the years to come. Remember, investing in your people is the most significant investment you can make for long-term organizational success.

Call to Action

This chapter has provided a framework for navigating the future of work. However, the specific strategies for your organization will depend on your unique industry, size, and culture. Here are some questions to consider as you move forward:

- What are the key skills and competencies your organization will need in the future?
- How can you create a culture of lifelong learning within your organization?
- What learning technologies can you leverage to enhance your workforce development efforts?
- How can you promote agility and adaptability within your workforce?
- How can you create a more inclusive and diverse work environment?

Conclusion: Investing in Your People, Investing in Your Future.

This book has explored the crucial role of workforce development in today's dynamic business landscape. We've delved into successful strategies for building a strong workforce, navigating common challenges, and preparing for the evolving future of work.

Key Takeaways:

- **Workforce development is a strategic investment:** It's not just about training employees; it's about empowering them to reach their full potential and drive organizational success.
- **A skilled and adaptable workforce is a competitive advantage:** By investing in your people, you equip them with the skills and knowledge needed to thrive in a constantly changing environment.
- **Continuous learning is essential:** The pace of change demands a commitment to lifelong learning. Organizations that foster a culture of learning will attract and retain top talent.
- **Effective workforce development requires a multi-pronged approach:** This includes identifying skill gaps, designing targeted training programs, measuring the impact of initiatives, and fostering a culture of continuous improvement.

Investing in Your Workforce: A Call to Action

Here are some actionable steps you can take to implement a successful workforce development strategy in your organization:

1. **Conduct a skills gap analysis:** Identify the skills currently possessed by your workforce and compare them to the skills needed for future success.
2. **Develop a learning and development plan:** Create a comprehensive plan that outlines specific goals, training programs, and development opportunities for your employees.
3. **Leverage technology:** Utilize online learning platforms, microlearning modules, and other technological tools to deliver engaging and accessible learning experiences.
4. **Empower managers:** Equip managers with the skills and resources to support employee development. Foster a culture of coaching, mentoring, and continuous feedback within your teams.

5. **Measure and track results:** Regularly evaluate the effectiveness of your workforce development programs through data collection and performance metrics.
6. **Promote a culture of learning:** Recognize and reward employees who demonstrate a commitment to continuous learning. Create a work environment that values growth, exploration, and innovation.

By following these steps and continuously investing in your workforce, you can cultivate a thriving, adaptable, and future-proof organization. Remember, the most valuable asset any company has is its people. Invest in them, and they will invest their talent and dedication in your success.

Thanks for your time.

www.ingramcontent.com/pod-product-compliance
Lightning Source LLC
Chambersburg PA
CBHW082213220526
45470CB00010B/3147